S0-BYC-037

What Others are Saying:

"I have worked with college students for over 25 years, and most of them are looking for ways to make money to offset the high cost of tuition in this economy. While many think they have to settle for minimum wage jobs at this stage in their lives, Tommy Bryant offers an alternative that provides the potential for much greater income while in college—starting your own 'dorm based' business!"

—Dr. Jim Nutter, professor

"This is great! We have all had moments when we wanted a 'Tommy in our pocket' as we spoke with other Gen Y's!"

—Stacey Turner, QNMD and Direct Marketer

"At last a down-to-earth tool to encourage the student who desires income while completing educational goals."

—Donald A. Garlock, EdD

"With a background of working for a Fortune 500 company for the past 30 years I have come to the realization that this is not our grandfather's corporate America. Gone are the days where there is a strong commitment between a company and the employee. Working in corporate America means you are trading time for money, that effort may not always equal re-

ward, that you will always have to answer to someone else, (whether it is a boss, a board of directors, or
the government.) It means you could get stuck in a
vicious cycle just trying to keep up with inflation or
the fear of termination, never able to build a independent future of your own. I wish I had a book like
Dorm-Based Business to inform me of the options of
how to build long lasting residual income. This book
is a game-changer!"

—K. D. Bennett
B.A. in Economics and Business Administration

"It is refreshing to see a young person strike such a
balance between effective business savvy and high
ethical standards. It is more than refreshing, it is in-
spirational. Look out Peter Drucker!"

—Pastor, United Methodist Church

"How exciting Tommy and Mary Lynn. Once it's out,
I will need to send this to my team members that are
in school."

—Sue Clark, Direct Marketer

DORM
BASED
BUSINESS

Direct Marketing
for Generation Y

by

Tommy Bryant

First Edition

Copyright © July 2010 by JP Revolution, LLC

All Rights Reserved. No part of this book may be reproduced or transmitted in any form or in any manner, electronic or mechanical, including photocopying, recording or by any information storage and retrieval system, without permission in writing by JP Revolution, LLC.

ISBN-1453686673
ISBN-13-9781453686676

JP Revolution, LLC
PO Box 4591
Lynchburg, VA 24502
(866) 637-3853

Editors: Mary Lynn Poe, B.S.; Sherri Ann Bennett, M.S.; Mary Lou Garlock, M.A.; The Rev. Dr. Thomas Bryant, Sr.; Dr. James H. Nutter.

Design by Donald A. Garlock, Jr.
www.dongarlock.com

Printed in the United States of America

www.dormbasedbusinessbook.com

Volume discounts available. Call (866) 637-3853.

To Katie

ACKNOWLEDGEMENTS

A special thanks goes out to everyone who helped me in writing this book:

To all my customers and team members who are the lifeblood of my business.

To the people who told me "No," for they have caused me to grow.

To my mentors in the areas of business, faith, and family, you know who you are.

To my friends.

To my family.

To my wonderful wife and best friend.

To the One who saved my life, Jesus Christ.

Table of Contents

FOREWORD

As a direct marketer for more than a decade, I personally know the struggles that come with building a home-based business. I was a stay-at-home mom with four young children. Raising kids, while developing an international network of distributors and customers, is not an easy task.

When my oldest son turned 18, he expressed interest in doing this business. I was eager to help him to be successful, but we realized that there was an entirely different set of struggles that he had to face as a college student. I became aware of the difficult circumstances that he experienced as a Gen Y-er that I did not have to face as a Gen X-er. Being taken seriously as a young adult was a huge hurdle.

Through trial and error, he figured out ways around these struggles working from his dorm room. At our international conferences, people were always surrounding him asking him to share his story and would he please talk to their Gen-Y teammates. He quickly realized that there was a need for this kind of book. His goal is to help others who are going through the same struggles that he had worked through.

Now that more and more young people are seeing the value in a home-based business, I wish that I had had this book when I was trying to help my son and other Gen Y-ers on my team. However, this book is not just for young direct marketers or their sponsors. I recommend this book to anyone who is seeking to make a home-based business successful.

I learned from my son as I read through this book. I could not be more proud of this young man who has integrity, character, and smarts about business at such a young age.

— MARY LYNN POE

INTRODUCTION

I didn't ask for any of this. I wasn't out searching for anything. I was just minding my own business and something bigger than I could imagine came along. It was neither a coincidence, nor did this book just fall into your lap.

You may be looking at the direct marketing industry because you are doing a research paper for school. A friend or a relative might have given you this book. Or you could have just been looking for the answer to a successful life. All are great reasons.

The reason I started my own home-based business was my Mom. She has been a direct marketer since I was 12. She has been very successful, but I never personally considered it as a serious career path. However, there was a shift in my thinking upon entering college. What I saw scared me; people paying lots of money for a degree, then working the rest of their lives just to get by, while having to pay off student loans. I certainly did not want that. I knew first hand the stresses of having a full-time job, going to school, and the pressure it puts on a family.

I started thinking: what if I didn't have to work for the rest of my life? What if I could be my own boss and work on my own schedule? Since that epiphany I have been transformed. I have passionately built my direct sales/network marketing business as a student since 2006. I have experienced first hand the many benefits of this business model. I am not just trading hours for dollars anymore; I am making a passive, or residual, income.

However, my Mom didn't spark this fire in me. It was a *third party*; much like this book is to you. I saw that she was successful, but I didn't really think I could do it until I saw that others were doing it at my age. When I realized that I, too, was capable, I started immediately. This is why I wrote this book: for you to realize the potential in yourself whenever the timing is right for you. We live in a new age of economic uncertainty. The best way to put a hedge of protection around yourself and your [future] family is to take matters into your own hands. Build a financial barrier that no person, company, or market can destroy. You can start *now* by building your own Dorm-Based Business without dropping out of school. *Now* is your time.

Just like a good company, this book has a mission statement. The goal is to achieve the mission with every reader:

To help as many young people as possible realize that they are capable of achieving their wildest dreams now, preventing them from ever getting started in the rat race of living paycheck to paycheck.

I hope these ideas connect with you the same way they did with me.

What is a home-based business?

A home-based business has many names: direct marketing, direct selling, network marketing, multi-level marketing, party-plan marketing, and person-to-person marketing. You can be called a distributor, an independent consultant, an affiliate or an associate. Just for consistency and simplicity, we will use Direct Marketing and Distributor throughout the book. The true definition could refer to any business operated out of the comfort of a home office, but we will be focusing on that which uses a unique distribution chain called direct distribution instead of traditional retail outlets. By not operating out of a storefront, we can save time, money, and energy for both the customer and the company. You will learn in this book why direct marketing is the wave of the future and why Gen Y-ers should consider starting their own home-based businesses.

What is Generation Y?

There are approximately 1.1 billion people (17% of the world's population) born from 1970 to 2000 who are considered a part of Generation Y. That is pretty significant. Yet, the majority of direct marketers are still from the other 83% of the population. This will soon change. As we get older there is more need for us to take over this growing industry. It is true that we are the future leaders of the world, but if we don't recognize the paradigm shifts that are going on around us, we are destined to fail by repeating the past.

This population group has seen its parent generation struggle to make ends meet while working more than ever. They've grown up with parents who experienced corporate layoffs, scandals, mergers, downsizing, market crashes, inflation, political chaos, and fraud. Generation Y knows that change is necessary. We want to work and live differently than our parents and grandparents. Now there is an avenue to make that change possible. We are already masters at networking because we have so many technological advances that allow us to stay connected with our surroundings. These are the same surroundings that our parents had that we now understand more deeply. You will learn in this book why the direct marketing industry revolution was made for Generation Y and why Generation Y was made for this industry. When the planets align like this, nothing can stop the momentum and the force will transform the world in years to come. As Victor Hugo said, "Nothing is as powerful as an idea whose time has come."

How To Use This Book

• Use this book as a reference, as a source. Hop around from chapter to chapter. You don't have to read cover to cover.

• Find one thing that works for you and use it. Doing this will make the small investment you made in this book worthwhile. If someone gave you an idea that sparked your imagination to create a new way of doing something that led to an extra $100 or even $1,000, how much would it be worth to you?

• Use this book to learn how to choose the right company, whom to talk to, what to say, and how to allow yourself to succeed in a business as a Gen Y-er. More importantly, it will help the process of transforming your thinking, because your mind is your greatest tool.

How *NOT* To Use This Book

• This is not a get-rich-quick book. Very rarely does anyone ever get rich quick with morality or standards. If someone tells you it is common, the method is typically at the expense of others. This is a get-rich-slow plan. Your wealth will be more stable, you will be helping people as you go, you will have it longer, and you won't be in jail. It's easier to make money outside of jail than inside.

• For Gen Y-ers who are not in college, this book is still for you. The basic principles are the same. In reading this book you will find that it doesn't really matter if you're in high school, college, graduate school, have a full time job already, or are retired. And you Baby Boomers and Gen X-er's who are sneaking a peek, you're welcome, too. You will learn all the basics of how to build your business in the most difficult circumstances and how to overcome them. But if you *really* want to you can skim over the parts that explicitly talk about campus events or dealing with your roommate, I can understand. Basically, the tips and tools you will learn in the book are not strictly for dorm-based businesses. You could have an apartment-based business, townhome/condo-based business, or even still-living-at-Mom-and-Dad's-home-based business.

- Disclaimer: This is not the only method that works. This is just what I have done that helped my team and me become successful. You may have plenty of other methods that work for you. In every venture in life, try a lot of things, keep what works, and throw out what doesn't.

Chapter 1

Industry Revolution

Don't you love those movies about time travel? I'm not a big sci-fi fan in general, but I love time travel, especially if the main character uses it to go back in time and manipulate the stock market and make millions! Man, if I could go back to 1986 (before I was born) and buy as much as I could of Apple, today I would be sitting pretty. Unfortunately, this is not possible and we have to use our own intuition for timing the market. Warren Buffett is a great example of being at the right place at the right time. He has amassed a fortune worth tens of billions of dollars just by purchasing the right businesses at the right time. He planned, prepared, and predicted the future. Of course, there was a bit of luck involved. Bill Gates had the right amount of talent, ambition, and the right amount of timing in the industry, and surrounded himself with the right people.

Many people believe that if they just do what these people did they will be rich, too. The truth is that there are too many young stock analysts and computer programmers looking to get into the industry with the same hopes and dreams. They may do well for themselves, but not like Gates and Buffett did. Why is this? What worked for those specific individuals at that exact point in history would not work again, at least not in the same way.

Let's look at it this way. If I told you that I'm going to start a cassette tape player company and the year is 2010, would you join me? Of course not! What if it were 1990? You may think that was a good time to invest since many were being sold at that point, but I would advise against it. Why? The market was saturated! That's why I would rather have started my tape player business in 1970. They were already on the market for almost a decade, and we know that records skip and get scratched easily, but those tapes don't and make for a great portable listening device. If you get involved in a movement before it takes off into the massive growth phase, but after the introduction phase, where it has already been tested out for a while in the marketplace, then you will experience the greatest return on your time and money.

The importance of "getting in early" also goes for the current distribution model of products. The Direct Sales industry is new enough that not everybody is using it yet, but we can predict that it will be what everyone uses in the future because it absolutely makes sense and the old way of a company getting products to the consumer is outdated. Timing is crucial to making the right decisions in business. Now you can't say that you've never been at the right place and the right time, like a Gates or a Buffett was.

Look at the flow of the following graph. The left side shows the traditional distribution method of products starting with the manufacturer who deals with the importing or exporting of parts to make the product. The product is then sent to a national distributor who marks it up and sells it to a regional distributor. Local wholesale venues take it from there and resell to a retail outlet or online store. On the right side of the graph the Manufacturer and the Direct Marketing company are the only two handlers before the product is sold to the consumer. This extra money saved will flow to each party involved in the process.

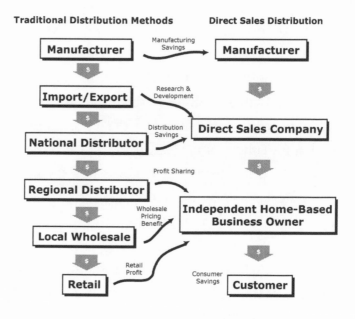

Direct marketing companies decrease the links in the chain of distribution, making it more efficient and cheaper for the end consumer. Think about how much extra money is spent on a product that costs only $10 to make. Because there are four or five middlemen, plus the advertising costs, the cost is $49.95 to the end consumer. Whereas, if a few of those people in the middle are cut out, the same quality product could be sold for $35 or less! Not to mention you are decreasing the carbon footprint by reducing the transportation of these products, back and forth. Efficiency always prevails, and that is why this will be the standard of distribution in decades to come. So, why join this revolution? What's in it for you? Most of the extra money that is saved goes straight to the independent distributor! This can help the people who take a step outside the box gain financial freedom and realize their dreams.

What's the catch? They have to be willing to be consistent, self-motivated, and willing to handle indifference. Understand that when the cassette tape came out, people still loved vinyl records and 8-tracks. When people started talking about these new, smaller plastic tapes for the first time, I'm sure that others laughed. Any new product or industry will have opposition in the beginning. The media and the public are not always on your side. So you must keep your chin up and be positive. Direct marketers have to wake up every morning and continue to promote their product or service, whether or not their friends, family, or the media support them. Those of you who are willing to handle adversity will be at the forefront of a business revolution. You, too, will reap the rewards of being 'in early' before critical mass occurs: like investing in a cassette tape company in 1970 instead of 1990. When everyone else has jumped on the bandwagon, listening to their cassette tapes, you can say your favorite phrase "I told you so" for them.

"One indication of the validity of a principle is the vigor and persistence with which it is opposed. In any field, if people see that an idea is obvious nonsense and easy to refute, they tend to ignore it. On the other hand if a principle is difficult to refute and it ... causes them to question some of their own basic assumptions with which their

names may be identified, they have to go out of their way to find something wrong with it."

— CHARLES OSGOOD

Advertising

If you've ever studied traditional marketing and advertising, you know that it can be costly. There are many forms of advertising including print, Internet, television, radio, signs, and mailings. They all make up a large portion, typically 30-40%, of a company's overall operating budget. Despite their large expense, the response ratio is quite low. Everyone can agree that the best form of advertising is word-of-mouth. The best part is that it's free! The buzz that goes from person to person the first weekend after a movie has hit the box office makes or breaks that movie. We do it every day when we forward a funny YouTube video or we tell a friend about our favorite new restaurant. When I first got Netflix, I was so excited about the concept, I told everyone about it, and never saw a dime from the company! What's great about direct marketing is that you just tell your friends and family about how

31

much you like your product. They get to decide for themselves; then you get paid.

Corporate America

Here's another part of the paradigm shift. What do most Gen X-ers and Baby Boomers say when you ask them how to increase your chances for success in life and be able to retire at age 65 with plenty of money to survive? Their answer is burned into their minds by society: "Study hard, get good grades, so you can get into a good school, and land a job at a big company with great benefits and a retirement plan." This worked for them at that point in history; however, it's not working for our generation. There are too many college graduates and not enough jobs for them. Employees are switching companies every few years. Countless longtime hard-working associates are being laid off and outsourced at random. The corporate culture, as we know it, is dissolving.

Many employees struggle with lack of time freedom. When you apply for a full-time position with any company you are signing away one-third of your weekday hours. It is sometimes very hard to take time off, especially when working for a larger company. Vacation time and sick days are being cut significantly. Ask corporate workers how often they wake up and feel like not going into work that day but have to anyway. For most, it happens often. I had the opportunity to work for a large insurance company one summer for four months. It was a great learning experience for me, looking back on it, but I dreaded every day of it. I had several different supervisors telling me what I was doing wrong and not in a nice way. I worked long hours and barely had an outside life, yet I wasn't getting ahead. I was only making the owner of the company rich.

However, in my own home-based business I am able to make more (per hour) than in my corporate job, work less, and also take off when I want to or not work at all for weeks at a time. It's that easy. People are getting fed up with having to report to someone who does not have *their* best interest at heart. The corporate philosophy is that if you don't perform up to par you're criticized until you do or you're fired. If they give you even a hint of praise, you will be thinking you are doing a good enough job and become complacent. It's a vicious cycle. If your teams of employees who work under you don't meet quotas or company standards, it's the same story. Who in the heck wants to live like this for the rest of life, with someone breathing down your neck at all times? This is why things are changing. More and more employees are becoming their own bosses.

The biggest advantage of staying in a corporate job is the health insurance benefits. I know many friends and family members who continue to work only because they need the medical coverage. What is most unfortunate is that recently a lot of companies are dropping these desired perks due to lack of funding. We all know that there are big political changes on the health insurance scene lately in America. Whether we agree with it or not, this aspect of our economy will be different in years to come, and we all need to properly prepare. The reason to stay with a company solely because of benefits is not a valid factor anymore.

We all have heard the sad but true stories of the big companies oppressing the little employee or small business owner. We all are familiar with the classic examples in recent decades of big companies falling out. When a company's management is greedy and has the ability to take advantage of people, unfortunately, sometimes they will. There is no regulation against this type of action other than pure and simple integrity until after the crime has been committed. Some management positions in these large corporations receive bonuses equal to the operating budget of a small company. Now, please know that I am not against someone earning a sum of money for a job well done. I just propose that there is a new mindset that will overcome this mantra, one that will enable everyone who is willing to take control of finances by becoming a part of the Direct Marketing industry. Welcome to the future of business.

Tax Advantages

One of the major benefits of owning a business is the tax write-offs. The government actually favors entrepreneurs by reducing their tax burden because they create jobs and fuel the economy. So Uncle Sam gives us a tax break! And that includes home-based entrepreneurs. If you make $500 or $1,000 dollars a month with your dorm based business and you spend 20% on dorm expense as part of your office, 10% on food when sharing your business, 15% on supplies including computer, paper, etc, and 15% on your phone bill, then the IRS actually lets you take that off of what you earned. So, in essence you only "made" 40% of your gross income. The only portion you have to pay taxes on is the net. Now, let's say you decided to get a job at the local campus coffee house and you get a whopping eight bucks an hour, if you're that lucky; 25% of that is taken off the top before you can even blink an eye. Then you pay expenses with what's leftover. When you own a business, you have more control. You pay yourself first, then the government. With a job you have to pay the government first, then you get your paycheck.

Please note: I am not a professional tax advisor. Consult a real one for your tax needs. I have an accountant who helps me plan my business taxes.

Benefits to You

- You get to work where, when, and with whom you want. Do you get to do that now?

- Leverage. You can use 1% of the efforts of 100 people and make more money with less time input than you would with 100% of your own.

- Low start up cost

- Low fixed expenses

- Path to quick profits

- Time Flexibility

Quick Facts

(Q) How many home-based businesses are there now?

(A) 35 million, approximately. That's almost double since 2000 and adding 8,500 daily.

(Q) Based on this, how many will there be in 2020?

(A) 66 million

(Q) What is the total annual sales amount of all the home-based businesses?

(A) $427 billion

Chapter 2

Grow Up Fast

Do you remember when you were a child and you were told you were too young to do something? I hated that feeling. I wanted to be an adult so fast. I wanted to have the freedom to do what I wanted when I wanted. However, we don't realize as children the responsibility that comes with being an independent adult. In college, most of us experience enough of the real world by being away from home. We like the freedom, but we don't want the responsibility that goes with it. Many people become stagnant and tend to prolong this stage of their lives for as long as possible until change is inevitable. Unfortunately, that is, many times, the reason why we take the five, six, or seven-year plan to complete a four-year undergraduate degree, changing majors more than we change socks. And that's fine for some people.

Of course there are some fields of study that require staying in school for longer periods of time. I'm not talking about those. I'm making reference to the many students who don't have an idea of what they want to do in life. This book is for you, because I was that way. Honestly, I didn't have a clue what I wanted to do until I found this business. As I have pursued my degree, I have racked up a substantial student debt. I hope that you may read this book and realize more what you want to do in life.

What I have learned in direct marketing, as a college student, is that we have to want to grow up fast. We have to get back to that feeling that we had when we were kids and we truly wanted to grow up. The majority of people who start a home-based business are between the ages of 35-55. At this point in life most have already finished school, had some career experience in at least one or two different fields, and even have a family. I'm not saying to do all that right before you start. I'm saying we have to change our mindset to realize why we need to start now at this age, instead of waiting until you've grown up enough. The best way is to simply start and you'll be taking a crash course in personal development just by doing this business.

You may be reading this book thinking it isn't for you because you don't want to "miss out" on your college experience. Your parents or other adults might tell you to enjoy these years because they will never be simpler. This is a sad cliché. It means that they are dissatisfied enough with their current situations to tell you that their college years were their best years. I believe with this business the best years of my life are yet to come. Each year of life will improve if you are constantly striving to tap into your full potential. So why wait to get the ball rolling? It will not happen over night, but at least you'll be making steps in the right direction. You'll be glad you did and so will the next generation.

Dealing with Your "Roommates"

Many times I had to wake up early, quietly put on a suit, and sneak out before my roommate woke up. You may have some resistance from your roommate in starting this business. You will probably have some problems with your roommate even if you don't start a business. These problems arise from just living with another person. I have come to use the term "roommate" as a figure of speech for any person who may not always affect you in the most positive of ways. This could be your spouse, family, friends, and teachers. It can even represent your own negative thinking. In this chapter, you will learn the best ways to deal with your many roommates.

Negative Peers

One day during my freshman year I was in my dorm office, connecting with new prospects over the phone. Another student who lived down the hall walked in my door. He had heard I was working on a business. He thought he was the expert on the subject and scornfully asked what it was.

"Isn't that a pyramid scheme?" he said. Without pausing I replied, "What is *that?*" Of course, I knew what he was implying. His intentions were to make me feel bad about it and maybe not do it anymore, in turn making him look good. But I also knew that he had no idea what he was talking about and could not further discuss the topic. All he knew was some headline on an ill-sourced blog or article that he found on the Internet.

Unfortunately, some people base their decisions on what they read on the Internet. Don't get me wrong. It can be a great source for some information, but a lot of it is false because anyone with a computer and connection can post something. He had no answer for me and asked me what it meant. I explained to him that just because something is shaped like a pyramid does not mean it is an illegal scheme. That's like saying triangles are bad and squares are good. Pyramid *schemes* are really called *ponzi* schemes and are illegal because there is no real product or service involved; just money exchanging hands at the expense of the new people who get involved.

These have been hidden in the form of a business plan, investment fund, or even a church.

Now, many things are shaped like a pyramid and are not schemes. In fact, it is the strongest structure known to man. Your family is a pyramid. Your school's faculty and staff are a pyramid. A church is a pyramid. People in Human Resources can tell you the intricate pyramid of the employees who work at a company. There are more folks at the bottom of the totem pole than VPs at the top. Corporate America is a pyramid. In any job you will be near the bottom of the pyramid until you work your way to the top. In the corporate world this "climbing" is a threat to the people above you, making it more difficult to find someone who has been on the journey to help you climb. But, in our industry of Direct Marketing, we only become successful if the people on our team are successful. So, naturally everybody wants to help each other be the best they can be. This makes for a super positive work environment.

Business organization can better be described as a funnel more so than a pyramid. In a regular company, you enter through the wide part of the funnel because the majority of Americans have a job, yet only a few make it through the funnel to the narrow part. There is only so much room at the top where the higher-level positions are. But in direct marketing it is completely the opposite. Only a few people at a time get to hear about us because we advertise through word-of-mouth marketing, which takes time and a lot of people. Once those people decide to enter the small end of the funnel, there is room for everyone at the top.

Negative Family Members

Family can be some of the most encouraging people and a great support system, but the same family can also be your worst enemies, when it comes to stepping out of the box and building your own business. Most of the time their intentions are good. They only want what's best for you. They did their best to make sure you had everything you needed in life to grow up in a healthy environment, get the best education, and live the fullest life. When they see something that could potentially hurt you they automatically create opinions for you and give advice. If you are getting negative feedback, check to see what they really mean. I used to get angry and assumed I knew the motive of what my family told me. Know that your family means well and don't take things personally. On the other hand, I get to work with certain family members including my Mom, who is actually my upline sponsor in the business. Definition: *An upline sponsor is the person who introduces you to your business, helps you get started, and serves as a mentor. I also have about 15 other family members involved on our team. Our business makes our relationships stronger.*

(Please note that not all situations are the same, you could have an extremely supportive family or no family at all. Each person comes from a different background and is unique. Use your individuality to help you in your business, not slow you down.)

Adult Prospects

Another form of age rejection can be from adult prospects. I remember an instance when I was still fairly new on the business-networking scene and showed up at a Chamber of Commerce event. I was ready with my nametag, business cards, and a short introduction for my business. I wasn't nervous, but I certainly wasn't completely comfortable in this setting. After working the room, meeting people and getting cards, I sat down next to a very professionally dressed woman. I introduced myself and proceeded to ask her about the company she represented. The first thing she said to me was that I was underdressed and if I wanted any respect from her and others I should buy nicer clothes. I was wearing a button down shirt with my company logo. My sleeves were rolled up because my arms are so long that most shirts don't fit me lengthwise. I had normal khakis and brown dress shoes on. I felt as if I dressed my best, considering my other clean shirt was a Super Mario t-shirt. I looked around the room and saw the other men were in suits and ties, but some had polos. Although I took offense at first and wasn't

47

sure what this woman was getting at, I took a deep breath, put on a smile, and said, "Thank you so much for saying that. I am always trying to improve myself. Because of your professional experience and expertise, I'm going to take your advice and apply it."

I could have completely blown her off and never talked to her again, but you never know who is going to be interested in your product or service. That is why you can't let negative emotions get in the way. Within a short time she turned out to be one of my faithful customers, a vast referral source that has led to many other great customers and team members, and a personal and business mentor. She even calls herself my Mom #2, and we get together often to catch up. I would have missed out on this relationship if I had let my pride get in the way. Even today when I know I'm going to see her I make sure I remember to slap on a tie.

Now, don't go spending a lot of money on "professional" clothes. Each line of business is going to have a different type of professional image. If you're a financial planner, selling insurance, or legal services, then business dress is appropriate. If you're selling cosmetics, you should always have neat hair and a flawless application of make up. If you represent nutritional products, try not to smoke or eat fast food, at least not in the presence of prospects. However, image can be taken overboard in the direct marketing industry. People will spend lots of money on nice cars, expensive clothes, and jewelry to make their business opportunity look more attractive. Their thinking is, "if I don't look like I'm rich, prospects are not going to think our compensation plan is lucrative." WRONG. The fact is: we are dealing with several different paradigm shifts in America today, not just the one of conventional employment versus direct marketing. The majority of people don't realize that having material luxuries is not a sure sign of wealth. In fact, most millionaires today don't drive expensive cars, buy big homes (which are liabilities, not assets), or try to "keep up with the Joneses." On the contrary, whatever the Joneses are doing, do the opposite! Going into debt to look good to prospects is a wrong motive. You don't want those people in your business anyway. We are younger, which usually means we don't have a lot of money.

You will find that those people want to look at your product or business because of you, not because of your material possessions. Those are the people with whom you want to work.

Chapter 3

Respect Your Elders, But Filter Their Advice

Don't let anyone make fun of you,
just because you are young.
Set an example for other followers
by what you say and do,
as well as by your love, faith, and purity.
— St. Paul from the 1ˢᵗ book of Timothy 4:12 CEV

Don't let these people get you down. When you feel insecure about being young, naïve, or inexperienced, take control of that fear. Do not let it control you. Fear can immobilize you and keep you from talking to new people. Understand that these people are probably dealing with insecurities, as well. Maybe they wish they could be as bold or innovative as you. Ask questions. Get them thinking about what is holding them back. You may learn more about them, yourself, or how to approach future prospects. You may even learn that they are actually interested in what you have to offer; they just don't know how to say it in a polite way.

When I first got started, and even to this day, I struggled with thoughts of insecurity. I thought that because of my age I would not be respected. Because I thought this way, it became my reality, even though it was false. The truth is, the moment those Gen X-ers and Baby Boomers see us walk in the room they are thinking about how much they would give to be able to start as early as we did. We know what we want now; they might not have had that privilege. Our ambition inspires them and attracts them to us. So if you ever have the feeling that you can't get customers or distributors or even approach your older, sometimes more successful business associates, remember how successful you already are because you are proactive about your financial future. You have time on your side, so take advantage of it.

Respect your elders without doing exactly what they did. Learn from the good; filter the bad. Nobody wins an argument. Wrestling with a pig only gets you and the pig dirty. The only problem is, the pig likes it. I do not mean to say that all your elders are pigs. The point here is that there are diplomatic ways of listening to the opinions and advice of others. Don't ever get mad at someone's opinion. It could be just a misinterpretation. If someone tells you to quit and stop wasting your life, then, stop and look at reality. Is what you're doing a good thing? If you are committed to your business and your belief is strong, then the answer is always "yes." Ask yourself a few questions about the sources of this person's comment:

· Is this person successful in this area of life?

· Is this a person who I would want to become more like? (Spiritually, emotionally, academically, financially, physically, mentally, socially?)

· Is this someone I trust? Someone who knows me and I know him/her?

· Is this person directly or indirectly paying my bills, making my decisions, or choosing the outcome of my life?

The answer is usually "no" to most, if not all, of these. Remember: we should never take advice from someone with whom we wouldn't trade places. Sometimes we get so wrapped up in what people say that we forget what originally brought us to the game. Go back to your 'Why,' which is your reason for getting starting in this type of business. Who do you want to be? What positive impact do you want to have on the world? We are all going to experience negative emotions from these kinds of situations, but the goal is to shorten the downtime from a couple weeks to a couple days, to a couple hours, to a couple minutes, then just a few seconds. Never again let anyone else determine the outcome of your life!

Don't Go To Parties

Okay, okay. I know some of you want to put down the book now. I'm not saying don't have fun. Do have fun. Enjoy your youth. Reward yourself for accomplishments along the way. I went to parties after a test or a big paper. It can be relaxing and a stress reliever. All I'm saying is to be careful of the crowd. That's right, I trust you. I don't trust the regulars, or the "party animals." I missed lots of parties because I knew the kind of people they attract. You want to hang around positive people because you become like the five people with whom you spend the most time. Think about those five people for a minute. Who are they? What does their lifestyle look like? What do they do for a living? How much do they make? Are you happy about becoming like these people?

If your answer is "No," you may need to revamp your list of people. The best way to do this is to get a mastermind group or a mentor. Find a few friends or acquaintances who have the same goals in life and maybe even the same vehicle to get those goals accomplished. Meet on a regular basis and talk about what you're going through and brainstorm different ways of getting the job done. This helps tremendously.

Rejection

After reading this section you might have a better glimpse of some of the situations you may face. You may decide that this business model is not for you. If rejection scares you enough to do nothing more than read this book, that's okay. This business model is not for *every*one. I will be the first to admit that. Although it's not for everyone, it is however for *any*one. The beauty of direct marketing is that it doesn't matter how old or young you are, where you live, where you came from, your race or sex, your educational background, or experience. There are no background checks, credit checks, interviews, and you don't have to supply a résumé or references.

Keep in mind, though, that rejection comes in many forms. If you are expecting to completely avoid it in life, well, you are out of luck. No matter what you do for a living or where you go, you will face rejection in one form or another. Whether it's from your teacher, your parents, your girlfriend/ boyfriend, your spouse, or from your boss, you are always going to be around negative people. It is inevitable. However, I would much rather be told by a prospect (even in the harshest way) that they don't want my product or business opportunity, than be told by my boss that I can't take off to see my wife and kids. I would rather be ridiculed by my peers now and live a life of freedom later, than conform to their ideas of working with them until age 65. No, thank you.

The best way to find out if direct marketing would be a good fit for you is to make a list of pros and cons. Good always outweighs bad. And remember, you can make money or you can make excuses, but you can't make both! Building a business can be the toughest thing you'll ever do. It will not be easy. It takes more work, longer hours, and extra effort on your part, not just for one day, but every single day until you get it off the ground and sustainable. A lot of personal growth is involved. But if the timing is right for you, none of that will matter. Nothing will get in the way of achieving your goals.

Chapter 4

Choosing the Right Company

Why would you spend all this time trying to become a better person if you do it with the wrong company? This next section is devoted to helping you decide which type of business opportunity is right for you. Choosing the right company from the beginning is very important because it's not the product or business you're selling; it's you. You are selling yourself to other people for their trust in you. A good reputation is crucial. If you align yourself with a company that has a corporate scandal then you become part of that image. You want to prevent every possible mishap by steering clear of bad business opportunities.

Note: If you are already involved with a company or you have an idea of the one you want to join, please don't skip over this section. You will either solidify your belief in that company, or decide that it's time to cut your losses and find a company that's a better fit.

Over the next couple chapters there is a point system to help you see if the company you are looking at meets these standards. Throughout this section you will find numbers with +'s and -'s. Start your clock at zero and keep track of the numbers as you go. If your number is fairly high, then you should seriously consider joining that company. If you end up with a low number or even a negative number, move on to the next company you are evaluating. Divide the total number you get by 42, and you will get a percentage that shows how well that particular company rates. This system covers various topics that make up a solid direct marketing company. It is not the "be all end all;" it is just a guideline.

Culture

There may be individuals you know who really love what they do, not just the ones who say it in front of their boss. I'm talking about the ones who eat, sleep, and breathe their company, club, or organization; who defend its values against anyone who dares speak out. They would rather die than switch to another company. We all know these fanatics. Surprisingly to many employees, money is not the top reason people love working for a certain company. It's the company's culture, the environment. The business culture is the overall experience you get while working with a company. Many companies have mottos, team colors, songs, special awards, recognition, secret handshakes, etc. as part of their uniqueness. You feel as if you are part of a greater cause when you work for a company with a positive work environment. If your first impression of the company you're looking at is not warm and inviting, I would hesitate. Of course, this is sometimes hard to measure from the outside so you'll have to go with your gut feeling.

· Culture welcoming, fun, unique, or you just liked it? +1

· Culture boring, unoriginal, nonexistent, or you just didn't like it? -1

"More than the money,
it's the person you become in the process."

— JIM ROHN

Training Program

One of the most important parts of choosing a company is the training program. If you have the best product and compensation plan, but no education from the company or your upline sponsors, then your chances of succeeding are slim. Many of the things you learn in direct marketing cannot be taught in a classroom. They must be learned through experience, action, trying and failing, and getting up to do it again. The emotional highs and lows of operating this type of business require that you have a support system in place. Not having that support team can be fatal to your business. There is a serious learning curve when starting your business, and if you don't have the shoulder of a mentor or corporate partner to lean on, you will miss the curve and get a bad taste in your mouth about the business in general. That is why I stress to make sure you will not be alone. Make sure that you will be in business *for* yourself, but not *by* yourself; that your sponsor, if you have one, is readily available to answer your questions, no matter how small, whenever and as long as you need help. This is what they are paid for; they will understand.

- Do you know who your sponsor will be? +1

- If not, -1

- Will (s)he be training and supporting you as you get started? +1

- If you are own your own, -1

- Make sure the company has a direct telephone line for product questions, as well as for placing orders. +1

- You'll want to see a distributor support department. How often are they available? How long does it take to reach a live person?

Also, you want to see how many different product lines the company has, the simpler the better. The learning curve for starting a business with a thousand products is longer than that of a business model that has just a few. Remember, it's better to sell one product to more people than different products to the same people.

Events

Another form of education would be live training events. Find out what the company offers in this area. These events are crucial and help move your business forward tremendously. Ideally, you want to see the company put on a couple of major international conferences a year. Put these at the top of your events priority list. If your company is doing things right, you should see the president and all the top corporate people there. The top leaders in the field should be presenting what they did the past six months and teaching others how to duplicate their success. You should also get to network with others, people who are out in the trenches everyday. These events show you that you're not alone. There should be trainings on a smaller scale that are close to home and less expensive. On an even smaller scale, there should be in home or local presentations that are done by you or your upline. These are done for prospects for the product or the business.

- Is there a guidebook that your company provides on how to do a home presentation on the product? +1

- Does the company have a manual or a go to resource for detailed questions? +1

- Does your company provide conference calls or webinars periodically? +1

- Does your local team have regular meetings for the product? +1

- For the business? +1

- Social gatherings, like a monthly potluck? +1

Commit to going to every event,
even if it means missing concerts
or athletic events.

Integrity

Make sure the company has integrity. If there is any hint of stealing, lying, cheating, or ill motives; run the other way. Sometimes it takes time to know if a company has a heart. The company I am aligned with made an incredible decision on the side of integrity that has reassured me that I am with a truly honest and giving organization. After hurricane Katrina hit the Gulf coast in 2005, the communities were devastated. However, the company sought out the customers wherever they were staying to make sure they received their product shipment, did not charge them, and paid the distributors as if the customers had paid for the product! Now, the company didn't make an announcement declaring this charity. The distributors in that area found out and shared their stories about this selfless act that affected them so much. Now that is integrity!

Check the company's background. Ask third-party friends or business associates who may know something about the company. Make sure it's a trusted source of information. Integrity is something hard to measure with points and is hard to know from the beginning. Usually, it's the gut feeling you have about the company. Trust your gut. There are, however, a few things you can look for:

· Does the company give back to the community through charitable organizations? +1

· Is the product or service something that truly influences customers in a positive way

+1

- Does it make the world a better place? +1

- When your sponsor or any other representative of the company speaks with you, are they focusing on themselves and what is best for them? -1

- Or are they looking at the needs of potential customers? +1

- Are they truly listening to you and what your goals are for the business? +1

- Do they have a mission statement? +1

- If not, -1

Track Record

It is important to study the company's history before joining. Make sure you know all their mistakes (and they all make them). What have they done to fix these mistakes and ensure they won't happen again?

A great resource for this research is the Direct Selling Association (DSA). It is like the Better Business Bureau for this industry. You can check them out at www.dsa.org

· Is this company a member of the DSA? +1

· No? -1

When was the company founded? You want to make sure it's a seasoned company, not an experiment with you as the guinea pig. That's why you should never get involved with a ground floor start up. These are typically the scams or the fly by night companies with a phony product. Make sure they have at least eight years of network marketing experience, not just in business, but specifically in this industry.

How long have they been successful in business with direct marketing?

- Less than 8 years or no direct marketing experience -3

- 8 to 15 years +1

- 15 to 39 years +2

- 40 or more years +3

- Debt free +1

Buyer's Club vs. Legitimate Business Opportunity

There are large buy-in-bulk grocery chains that are buyer's clubs. You pay X amount of dollars per year to get discounted products. You save money on products, but you're still spending it. They don't send you a check. Unfortunately, a lot of direct selling companies are simply just buyer's clubs. You don't want to get involved in one. There is little opportunity to make money. It's more of a hobby and not a profitable business.

Also, if it is a buyer's club, that means you'll have to approach more people about the business. Not everybody wants to join your business, but everyone needs your product, if you've chosen the right product to represent, of course. Don't enable your prospects to throw out the baby (product) with the bath water (opportunity).

Now don't ask your potential sponsor point blank if it's a buyer's club. That person might deny it just to get you in. In fact, it is not necessary to inform the person that you are investigating. Ask for the facts and do your own research into the company.

What percent of consumers of the product are just customers and what percent are distributors?

- 50% distributors or more -2

- 16 to 49% -1

- 15% or less +1

Corporate Leadership

- Can you talk to the president +1

- Without feeling degraded? +1

- Does the founder(s) have a background in direct selling? +1

- Have they started one or more other network marketing companies before this one? -1

That's another bad sign of company hopping.

Field Leadership

Who would your upline sponsor be? Do an interview to make sure it's someone you see yourself working with for potentially the rest of your life. Remember, you get to choose who you want to work with in this business.

- Do you like your upline? +1,

- If not, can you find another in that company who you do like?

- Are there people who are still making it to the top level of the company on a yearly basis? +1

- Or has there been a long gap of several years since the last one? -1

Investment

What is the company doing for the money that you pay to them? What's great about direct marketing is that it's low investment, but how much are you getting for your buck? Weigh the cost of getting involved with how much you get in terms of services, marketing materials, and support that you receive for that investment. For instance, the company I work for:

- Takes customer's orders

- Ships product directly to the customer

- Sends a welcome letter, follow up emails, and periodic newsletters

- Provides a starter kit with promotional CDs and DVDs

- Provides regular, local product and business events

- Hosts two annual International conferences

- Has a distributor support call center, an online virtual office, and an individual product website

- Handles my personal accounting and sends me reports

- Creates cash bonus incentives and recognizes achievement

- Releases new marketing programs

- Invoices and collects payments from customer

74

- Then PAYS ME and my downline

- All of this for $50 a year!

If your initial investment is several hundred to a thousand dollars or more, find out how that money is used.

- Does your sponsor get paid from that for merely signing you up? -1

- Or do you actually have to sell some product to start making money? +1

Chapter 5

The Product

Timing

Let's get back to the cassette tapes analogy: you don't want to get involved with a company that is new to a product or one in which the market is completely saturated. The best time to get involved is somewhere in between. If you get in too early, it is very risky and might be a flop. Yet, you want to be in early enough that you experience the growth phase, but know that the product is tried and proven. Look at this common product lifecycle chart. The best point to get involved with any product is where the arrow is.

Product Lifecycle

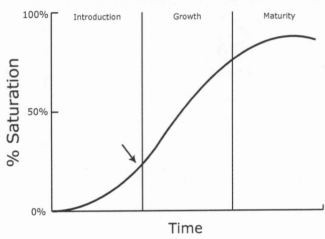

Do some research. Where does your product place on the S curve? What is its saturation level in the market place?

· 90% or more -1

· 20-89% +1

· 1-19% +2
· less than 1% -1

Inventory

In the old days of direct marketing you actually had to purchase the entire inventory. Unfortunately, this left a lot of people with garages full of unsold product. Today, some companies ship your customers' products directly to them, saving you the hassle of running around town and the risk of not being able to sell all your products before the expiration date. Keep in mind: this may not apply to all products or services.

· Inventory? -1

· Direct ship? +1

Market Place Success

Is there a widespread need for the product? Everybody should be a candidate for your product. You don't want to go through the day and find anyone who couldn't be a prospect. Now that doesn't mean everyone is going to buy your product; that just means that everyone is a potential purchaser. For example, if you had a product that helped clean dentures, your target audience would be only people who had dentures. How many people do you talk to everyday who wear dentures? Even if they did, would you want to ask them?!

· Everyone? +1

· Only a specific market? -1

Is the media backing the product? It's important that you are not the only person or company out there explaining why there is a need for your product. You want the media preaching your message so you can use it as third party validation. Many people get discouraged when they see other companies compete with their product. Competition is a great sign because it shows a consumer need, that many people are concerned about the same issues, and that there are other advocates for it. Now all that remains is to show them how you are different and why your product is the best!

· Media? +1

· Competition? +1

Is it sold in stores? If so, find you may need to find something more unique. The product needs to be one-of-a-kind. There should be nothing else like it. The people promoting the product should be satisfied and loyal customers first, who can share from the heart why they love it, not store clerks whom only care about when their shift ends. A retail outlet's main selling point is usually price, whereas, direct marketing is based on relationships and trust.

· In retail outlets? -1

Is it a one-time purchase or is it consumable? There are a lot of products out there today. A good majority of them are products that you buy once and don't need again for a while, if ever. This is not the kind of product you want to sell because you only make that money once. The residual income kicks in when you have a product where people are constantly running out of their supply and they need to come back to you for more. You want to be known as the go-to guy or gal for this product.

This takes time, but the longer you are involved the bigger your network of users becomes.

· Consumable? +1

· Not? -1

You have to be a product of the product. You have to be consuming this product if you want to sell it. No questions asked. People are going to ask if you take it, own it, or use it. If you don't, they will know and whatever your reasons for not owning it will become theirs as well. And if you're not interested enough to buy it yourself then you probably should not sell it.

Chapter 6

The Business

Territory Restrictions

The traditional direct selling way is to have predetermined areas where you can do your business exclusively. No one else can do that business in your territory and vice versa. You do not want to get involved with a company that restricts you from doing business in certain parts of the state, country, or world. This prevents you from expanding your portable business. It's especially a detractor to college students because your college friends are usually from various places.

The world, in general, is getting smaller; with technology, we can connect with people farther away faster than we ever could before. This is why any company with territory restrictions is an outdated form of doing business.

- Territories? -1

- None? +1

Income Potential

Look for immediate and long-term income. To benefit your wallet in the best way, you want to find a company that you can make money immediately, not one that takes years to make a profit (like most conventional, bricks and mortar businesses.) You also want to have a stable and lasting residual income. You want the right combination of both because in the beginning you are going to be working a whole lot longer and harder due to the learning curve. You want to compensate for this curve by earning a more stable income. Be sure you can make money from several different parts of the compensation plan. What is the retail profit? What type of commissions can you make on your orders, and your downline's? And what about bonuses?

Downline: Anyone on your team whether personally sponsored by you or anyone else on your team. Each degree of separation is called a generation.

On how many generations down can you earn profit?

- 3-5? +1

- 2 or less? -1

- Ask: Can I make money just selling the product? +1 How much?

This is important because most people don't want to recruit others. If you truly have a legitimate and lucrative business plan you should be able to make a good amount of money just selling the product.

Quotas vs. Cumulative Volume

Some companies have sales quotas, which means you have to sell a minimum amount every month to maintain your business. This is not good for the part-timer or the college student. Most people start in business part-time, and this model eliminates a lot of potential prospects. Even for full-timers this can be hard because you may talk to a lot of people one month, but they might not pan out into sales until the next month. When you work with the decisions of other people, you can never predict the exact amount of response. Look for a company that allows you to qualify for position advancements with cumulative volume over time, not just in one month.

· Quotas? -1

· Cumulative volume? +1

Another question to ask is, once you get to these positions are you liable to lose your title if you don't maintain the volume of sales that got you there?

86

Compensation Plan

You don't want a company to take away your commission level once you have worked hard to attain it:

- Are the positions all permanent? +1

- Position requalification? -1

- Is your business inheritable to your future heirs? +1

Don't worry so much about the different compensation plans; just look for a few major things. Ask if the compensation plan is *binary*. This means that you only have two possible lines, and everyone you sponsor has to be placed in one of those two lines. This will limit your income potential but give more to the company. You want to make sure there is no limit to the number of people you can recruit frontline or direct to you, which is called *unilevel*.

- Binary? -1

- Unilevel? +1

Beware of Scams

Unfortunately, there are a lot of dishonest people out there trying to cheat others out of money. The same is true in this business. There are many "work from home" schemes that you see on the Internet, usually through spam emails, Internet ads, newspaper ads, and TV infomercials. Sometimes they can be in the form of real live con artists, but this is a dying breed. Most scammers are afraid to show their faces. Don't fall for the hype of a sales person. If it seems to be sketchy, sleazy, or a scam, it probably is. If they claim to make you $100,000 your first month or even $5,000, don't believe it. These are key phrase indicators of a fake business scam:

- No selling.

- Make money while you sleep.

· Guaranteed income.

· Easy or no work

Now, divide your number by 42 and multiply by 100%. If the score is something you would be okay with for a quiz grade in class, then you should look into joining the company. If the score is 60%, or less, consider why and do more research, but it doesn't necessarily mean that it's a bad company. If you have a negative score, I recommend declining that company.

Have questions about evaluating a company or can't decide on one? We are happy to answer any questions not mentioned here. Please email us at DormBasedBusinessBook@gmail.com

Chapter 7

Marketing Yourself

Now that you've chosen a company and signed on as a business owner, it's time to learn how to do the business successfully as a student or someone in their 20-somethings. The concepts are very simple to grasp but it takes a new mindset, patience, persistence, and consistency to apply them. I know you are completely capable because you've made it this far. Let's get started.

Tell Your Story

Your story is your 30-second elevator pitch/ commercial that you tell everyone. If you just wing it, you might forget some important details or you might go overboard and verbally vomit on someone. This scares people away. So, know your story well and tell it often. A good story includes:

· Your name and your company.

· A brief description of your product or service in the form of an "I help people _____ with _____" statement. For example, if I were representing a product that increased gas mileage in cars I would want to say after the question, "What do you do?," "Well, you know how gas prices are on the rise and people just can't afford it anymore. Well, I help people increase the gas mileage of their current car by just adding Liqa-mile to their gas tanks."

· Ask them if they would be *open* to more information. No one is going to say, "No, I am closed-minded."

- Use a win-win question. "Would you rather watch a DVD or listen to a CD?"

- Be sure to set a follow-up appointment if they are interested. This helps you clearly define the logical next steps for the prospect. If you call without an appointment you could face more rejection than if they were expecting your call.

Memory Jogger

A Memory Jogger is a complete list of everyone you know. Do this first when you open your business. This should be in the 250-500 range for most older adult generations, but for us Gen Y-ers it's significantly less because we've only been on the planet for so long. But you, the dorm-based business owner, will have many more names than the average person, just because of your newly acquired ability to network.

When you are writing your Memory Jogger you don't want to prejudge anyone. That means that if there is someone you think won't be interested, still write their name. I have been quite surprised by some of the people I thought for sure would say "no" but said "yes," and vice versa.

You will have a portion of your Memory Jogger called your *chicken list*. These are the people who may intimidate you, or maybe you just don't know them that well and you're afraid they'll reject you. Everyone has a chicken list. The best thing to do is call those people first. You'll be glad you did. It will make every other name on the list much easier. You never know who will say "yes," and it could be one of your chicken list people.

Speaking of chicken lists, my sponsor in my business is my Mom. Her sponsor is my aunt, her sister. My aunt was on the chicken list of her sponsor for TWO whole years. Yet, as soon as her sponsor called her, she signed on not only as a customer but also as a distributor on the same day. Within five years my aunt reached the top level of the company. Think of this: what if my aunt's sponsor chickened out and never called her chicken list? My aunt would neither be where she is today, nor my Mom, nor I. Which means you would not be reading this book because it would not exist. So for the sake of all the people that you may never know, but may change their lives, don't hesitate to talk to everyone. Everyone you know deserves a chance to hear your message. It could change their life and the lives of many others, and you will get paid handsomely for it.

"Say less to more people."

Many people get caught up in talking a long time to one person who may not be that interested. Since they don't know what you know about your product, you feel the need to convince them. I would advise against this. Arguing with one person keeps you from talking to many more people. What do you accomplish by this? You're only wasting precious time that could be spent talking to the next person. Instead, politely exit the conversation and move on. For instance, a leader in our company looks at her business as if it's a long line that goes into infinity. She asks each one, not wasting any time on one prospect. She tells her same story to each. If someone says "Yes," she pulls that person out of line and works with that individual. If someone says "No," she says, "Next" and that person goes to the back of the line, because "No" really means "Not right now, the timing is wrong." Don't completely forget about these people because I've had a lot of old prospects change their minds and decide that now is the right time.

Find a Buddy

The best way to successfully run a business is to find a buddy. When you first get started with your business you have a fresh excitement. All you want to do is talk, eat, sleep, and breathe your business. You want to find someone who is just as obsessed about it as you. Lock arms with that person, and this business will be a whole lot easier. Handling rejection seems more possible when you have your buddy.

This doesn't mean that you have to stick to one buddy. You could have several. And they could have different ones, too. Your buddy might not be same person every year. Be prepared that your best friend from childhood or even your best friend now may not be interested in the least in what you're doing. This lack of support can cause a rupture in any relationship. Friends come and go. The friends you have now may not be the same ones that you will need as you start this new path in life.

Because I was 18 when I started my business, I had few candidates for this type of buddy. My Mom was my first buddy and still is a great one today. My best friend from grade school was a buddy for about a year and then dropped out of the business to pursue other ventures. Life happens to people and timing is not always right. Don't take offense.

Build Lasting Relationships

It is so important for us to create good relationships with the people around us. Long-term relationships equal long-term success. Since we are young, we have a longer time to build more relationships and to develop the ones we've already got! The larger your contact base, the more people you are affecting in a positive way, and the more money you will make as a result.

Try not to burn bridges. Sometimes certain people can unknowingly get on our last nerve or even do something that is hurtful. It's important to at least maintain contact because you never know who they may become or what they might do for a living. You may need to reconnect with them at some point in the future. Chances are they have forgotten all about the situation that made you want to burn the bridge.

Always be looking for the best in people because their best will come out in the form of action. You never know who can be a super star in your business. It's a good life quality to have anyway.

Be the Best Distributor on Your Team

What does the best team member look like? (S)he's the person who has the most distributors, the most customers, who comes to every event with people, and who has the best attitude. If you strive to be this person, your team will see that and follow your example, creating even more activity and momentum. Prospects are attracted to this and will want to join your team over any other team in the company.

Share, Not Sell

I encourage you to do some research and self education in the area of selling. When I started my business, I read books on selling, marketing, prospecting, and closing. I always have a set of audiobooks in my car or on my iPod. Listen or read something like this for at least an hour a day. Even today, I fall asleep listening to something on my iPod and then I wake up and read something positive. This practice keeps me in check because so many times we can get sidetracked. Keep in mind, our business is completely different from conventional businesses; especially those that require commission only salespeople to cold call (trying to sell to a stranger) and hard close (applying excessive pressure on a prospect to buy the product). This is the old way of selling. What we do in direct marketing today is simply sharing. Some of the information that you get from these sales training tools may need to be tweaked a little. Here are some simple tips on how to be a good shareperson:

1. Meet new people every day

2. Make friends, lots of them

3. Remember people's names and use them often

4. Be nice to everyone you meet

5. Ask questions. Don't talk about yourself too much
    i. Find out what they do, like, care about

ii. Ask for their business card. It's more important that you have theirs than for them to have yours, but that doesn't mean to refuse to give yours to them!

6. Use "back door marketing" - creative, non-confrontational ways to tell people about your product.

7. When someone says "No," ask who they know who might be interested.

Invite, Not Recruit

The same concept is used when people are joining your business. Share the business with people and invite them to join your team. Don't pressure them by guilt or scaring them.

People often say to me that the economy is too poor to get started in the business. In reality, that's actually the best time to build your team because more people are hurting for money. By the time the economy picks up you will have a running team to catch all those customers. Learn to *capitalize* on the inevitable business cycle, not *complain* about it.

Chapter 8

Useful Verbiage

Sometimes it can be difficult getting our message across to people being a Gen Y-er. Have you already tried doing what your upline told you to do, but it didn't work in your situation? There is a difference in communication between you and your college friends, high school friends, parents of friends, family, and other adults. This next section will teach you how to communicate with each of these groups.

How to Talk to People on a College Campus

People you already know — let them know what you just started doing and how excited you are about it. If you have been doing it for a while, that's okay. You can tell them you've restarted.

People you meet as you go — most will ask what your major is or possibly about your interests. If your major relates to your business, weave it in by saying, "I'm studying ___, but I'm putting it to use right now by ___." If it doesn't, that's fine too. "My major is ___, but what I really enjoy doing is working ___ out of my dorm room." Please feel free to use the title of the book and say, "I own my own Dorm-Based Business."

You will probably hear this more than anything else from our age group: I'm looking for work. Part-time employment was practically made for the student and young person. That's your perfect opportunity to tell them that your company is hiring.

After all of these things you'll want to ask if they'd be open to talking more about it over coffee. Set an appointment. If they are interested, but not enough to meet with you, just tell them to check out your website.

How to Talk to Your Old High School Friends

The best time to talk to your high school friends is when you're home on a break. Take a couple hours and call everyone you know using the same script. "Hey ___ It's _____ from high school. How's it going? How is school? Listen, I'm really excited about a business I just started and I wanted to get your opinion on it. (Relate it to something you may have in common or something you may know about them). Is there a time when we could get together at Starbucks?" Every time I was home from college I booked up my schedule in two-hour blocks to allow time enough to meet and to travel to the next place. 9am, 11am, 1pm, 3pm, 5pm, 7pm, 9pm. No, I didn't work 12 hour days because not all the spots were taken, and there will be quite a few no-shows and cancellations. It's just the nature of the business. Also, it didn't feel like work anyway. I was just hanging out and catching up with old friends. Note: This is a good way to set up your schedule for all your appointments. Of course, you'll have to work around class and other regular meetings, but the overall concept is the same.

Strangers

Any new person you meet, whether it be on the street, in a networking meeting, or friends of friends at a social event, you should introduce yourself as a part of the company you represent. Most people typically ask what you do or if you go to school and what you're studying, especially older folks. They are trying to be nice and it's a common question. I encourage you to steer the conversation away from that. I'm not saying to lie to people or avoid their questions, but when asked what you do you have the choice to bring up anything you do. Most people default to the safest thing. Either, "I'm a student," or "I'm in sales." The first statement will make them ask questions about school. You want to focus on your business. The second is a dead-end statement and will not intrigue the person to ask any more. I consider these *cop-outs*. Instead, be creative and try to direct any question to your product or your business. Then go into your "I help" statement (from page 92) and possibly your story.

How to Approach Professors, Parents of Your Friends, and Other Adults

Some adults may be more intimidating than others. I don't find the people in my business networking groups intimidating because most of the time they are looking for the same thing I am and are much more accepting of me. However, the adults who knew you as a kid or parents of your friends, for instance, can be down right scary to approach. Why is this? My feelings were that since they knew me as a kid then that's all I would ever be to them. However, this is hardly the case. It is only that way in our own minds and it takes a mind transformation to look at the situation in a positive light.

Also, the professor-student relationship tends to be a poor foundation for a successful business transaction. They are paid to help you learn a subject, pass a course, and eventually graduate, in the process making you better-equipped to handle the "real world." When you approach them in any way outside of this intended relationship you can catch them off-guard and the situation could become awkward. I'm not saying don't go for these contacts, because I've see many teachers and professors become master direct marketers because of their experience in teaching and leading others. But in my experience, professors at the college level, depending on their field, are not interested in dealing with businesses. There are simple ways to make you feel more confident and less tense while approaching any adult.

You know what you know about your products and business. If fact, YOU are the expert because you know more than they do about your business, but you can't act that way because that is arrogant. You have to *pretend* that these people in your life know everything there is to know. They are the wisest, most experienced, most successful, most educated, coolest, nicest people. And they may be; don't get me wrong. They just need a little extra boost or incentive to open their ears and let their barriers down. Relate to them what you have to offer. Show them how much they have meant to you in the past. Bring up specific examples of how they helped you learn a valuable lesson. Just make it known to them that you trust them as a source of good advice; a person in whom you can confide. Use phrases such as, "I wanted to get your opinion on this," "Your feedback is very important to me," and "I need your help with taking a look at this, can you help me?" And who could say "No" if you added a puppy face in the mix?!?

You also want to be able to relate something about what you are now doing to their experience. For instance, several of the contacts from my childhood are in business for themselves. One of them was even my boss at one time. I simply used what I knew about his field of expertise and related it to my business. "Mr. Boss, with your background in business and all the experience you've had running this place, I'd love for you tell me what you think about this business I've started." Your prospect could be an expert in your product field. This person could be someone who is highly respected and is always being sought after for sound wisdom.

All of these things build up ego in a positive way. People tend to be more open to what you have to say. It doesn't mean that each one is going to join you in business or even have something nice to say, but it means you are doing your job. You are successfully getting your message out to open ears in the most effective and efficient way. Because you are doing this, no matter how people react to your request, you will find those specific individuals who are right for your product or your business. They will know it from the start. It has been said, "You can't say the right thing to the wrong person and you can't say the wrong thing to the right person." Basically, people are going to do what they are going to do regardless of how you persuade them. It's just a matter of whether you do your job or not, and tell them what you have to offer. Don't worry if you screw up and say the wrong thing, because the right person will get the message anyway. No matter how hard you try and how many things you say, if it's not the right person, then it won't work out anyway.

Employ Your Upline, after all that's what they're paid for.

Your upline sponsor in the business wants to help you succeed. Never feel bad that you need help or want to share a success you had. Make sure you are using their expertise in every way you can.

Ask your sponsor to do three-way calls. When you have a prospect who is not impressed by your success story, do a three-way call with your upline. Introduce the two on the phone with the highest of praise for each other and let your sponsor do the magic.

When you decide that you want to start having events, let your sponsor know. He or she will be happy to help you coordinate that event, set up a speaker and room, and invite.

When I get discouraged in my business, and I still do to this day, I call my upline to share experiences and get encouragement. If I don't find what I'm looking for or need to hear, I keep going upline or sideline until I do. Remember to take advice from any person with a grain of salt. Find someone who is most like you would want to be and ask for advice. Not everyone will be the perfect mentor in every area. You might need to have several different mentors to cover all your bases. The most important thing to remember is NEVER WHINE DOWN LINE. If you have a complaint, or a not so positive remark, never tell your downline; always go upline. This can affect your downline in a negative way, but your upline can handle it because they've been there before. And their sponsor has been where yours has been and so on and so on until the president of the company. Someone will always be there to help give advice.

Reaching Out Off-Campus

Understand that the majority of your qualified prospects might not come from campus; you may have to look elsewhere. It's good to talk to everyone you know. That means to start with people on campus and old school friends. Eventually you will dry up that market. When this happened to me I went off campus to where people do business. I started visiting networking groups like BNI, the local Chamber of Commerce, Rotary Club, Kiwanis, Jaycees, Toastmasters, Retail Merchants Association, etc. There are lots of groups designed to help you meet more people and present your business. That is exactly what you need.

I have typed a script for what I say to networking groups. It is in an article specifically for the company I am with, but it could be easily translated. If you are interested, I would be happy to email you the Word document. Send an email to: DormBasedBusinessBook@gmail.com with a "Networking Script" in the subject line.

The following graph represents the age range of my customers versus my distributors. This is real-life data pulled from my personal business. Hopefully, this will help you see where you should

Age Range

Customers vs. **Distributors**

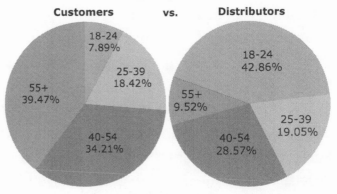

focus your efforts for the product and your efforts for the business. The key is to talk to everyone you can because if you skip over any one of these age groups, you will be missing out on potential business.

114

Chapter 9

Building Events on Campus

Most home-based businesses have something called a party plan. The bulk of meetings held are informal, social meetings in the home. These can be fun to attend and a great business booster. This makes it hard for dorm-based business owners. A dorm room is not the ideal place to invite people who don't live on campus. Another down side is space. It can be embarrassing to some, but others make it work. You could have a group of campus friends over, but it is often easier to use public places or the homes of others. You're going to want to have your presentation portable. Take your laptop to Starbucks or a restaurant. There are many public places on campus that allow students to congregate and even use multimedia equipment. My first big event was during my second semester of college. I was in a new market, as my company was not very well known in that city yet. I asked the event coordinator of the college who handles renting out the rooms. My school allowed students to use rooms for free. I just had to schedule the time. A leader in my upline was willing to drive a distance and do the lecture for me; all I had to do was get "butts in seats." I planned for this event with all my energy. I had over 250 contacts during the past six months and I called every one to personally invite them to this event. Most of them I had met in the business networking setting, so naturally they were excited about the potential to network with other business people. One hundred of those RSVP'd with a "yes." Only thirty-five showed up. I was discouraged at first, but that's just the law of averages. I later found out that thirty-five was a great attendance for a first lecture in a new city. This was a product only lecture. Never have a business opportunity lecture where you invite people who have never heard of the product first. It's always best to lead with the product, not with the business opportunity. Save the business opportunity presentation for a one-on-one or a small group of people who know what to expect.

Inviting

It's important to use the call-send-call method when building for events because it's the most proven way to get people there. Email blasts and even Facebook event pages don't work as effectively by themselves. I called every one personally, encouraging them to come with me. Then I sent out either a flier in the mail or an email with details and directions. The most important part is the reminder call. This is typically 24-48 hours before the event. Call every single one that you called the first time and ask if they will be there. You get a 30-40% response rate using this method, whereas, you only get a 1-2% response rate from email, Facebook blasts, radio, television advertising, or posting fliers around campus.

Make Sure Your Event is Professional

- Have music playing before and after while people are networking.

- Bring door prizes and give everyone a raffle ticket.

- Have everyone sign in for proper follow-up.

- Introduce your speaker.

- Ask people to turn of cell phones and let them know where to find restrooms.

- Bring a gift for the speaker and give it after the presentation.

- Dress professionally. Suit and ties for guys. Business attire for ladies.

- Possibly refreshments.

Capitalize on the Follow-Up After an Event

Following up with everyone in a couple days after the event brings the most results from an event.

For those who came:

- Thank them again.

- See if they are still interested in your product. If not, ask them if they know anybody who would be.

- Let them know about the next event.

For those who didn't show up:

Don't be discouraged because this is the best part. You may have a lot more people who said they were going to come but didn't, versus those who actually show up. This means you have a lot more people who are feeling bad that they missed it. They went back on their word and feel guilty.

They almost "owe you one." Well, this is your chance to "cash in" on that favor. Tell them how great a time everyone had at the event and about the fabulous information that they missed. They will apologize profusely. You just tell them you would be happy to catch them up on the information on a one-to-one basis over coffee. Set an appointment and do a mobile presentation for them. I tend to get more customers from the group that didn't show up than the ones who did! Once you have a team of distributors promoting for events just as you do, your business will explode exponentially.

Chapter 10

Envisioning

Find out what your 'Why' is. What gets you motivated? Why do you want to make this change? What keeps you up at night? What gets you up early? Can you see the big picture? Can you see how much of a difference you can make in your life and in the lives of your future family, children and grandchildren? Maybe there is some goal you've always wanted to achieve. Is this going to be your vehicle to get you there? Is there something that makes you wish your family had done more to be successful? Go out there; be the change in your family legacy.

I developed my why before I started my direct marketing business. I knew enough about what I didn't want in life to determine the basis of what I did want. My why is to build a stable income to support my wife and kids comfortably, without working long hours and missing my kids growing up. I want to be able to take off when I want to spend time with my family. Of course, at the time I didn't have a family, but now I am married. It is the most fulfilling activity to sit down with my wife and plan what we want for our future.

The most fun part of this business is dreaming. You can see the light at the end of the tunnel, unlike so many regular jobs. Provided that you have chosen the right company and you plug into the system, you have the potential for unlimited income. That's right, there is no cap on how much you can make with this business model. So when is the best time to get started? NOW. The time is always now. If you wait until school ends or until you drop a certain class, you're going to miss the boat. The money is made only by the people who take action.

"If you don't see the big picture,
you won't do the small steps to get there."

What's your big picture? You already know the small steps to get there. They are laid out for you in this book; but it's all worthless if you don't envision yourself as someone who has already achieved success with your own dorm-based business. Why would you want to do this business? Let's dive a little deeper and find out exactly what your goals are.

Goal setting worksheet

Change is inevitable; growth is optional.
All barriers are self imposed.

Goals must be...
    Written
        Specific
            Have a Time Limit

In the book *What They Don't Teach You in the Harvard Business School*, Mark McCormack tells of a study conducted with students in the 1979 Harvard MBA program. In that year, the students were asked, "Have you set clear, written goals for your future and made plans to accomplish them?" Only three percent of the graduates had written goals and plans; 13 percent had goals, but they were not in writing; and a whopping 84 percent had no specific goals at all.

Ten years later, the members of the class were interviewed again, and the findings, while somewhat predictable, were nonetheless astonishing. The 13 percent of the class who had goals were earning, on average, twice as much as the 84 percent who had no goals at all. And what about the three percent who had clear, written goals? They were earning, on average, ten times as much as the other 97 percent put together.

Source: http://www.lifemastering.com/en/harvard_school.html

What is my purpose for starting my dorm-based business?

_____

_____

_____

_____

When would I like this to happen?

_____

How will these things change my life?

_____

_____

What am I willing to do on a daily basis to make this happen?

_____

_____

_____

_____

How much am I going to be making in 3-5 years?

_____

How would 'making a difference' change my life?

_____

How would more money change my life?

_____

How would more time freedom change my life?

_____

How many hours a week can I set aside to begin achieving my goals?

Employ yourself. Remember: You have no boss, so your company is not going to call you and see if you're working. It's up to you to talk to people.

How many times are you willing to fail before you achieve your dreams? If you answer this question with a number, then your 'why' is not strong enough. Thomas Edison failed over 10,000 times before inventing the light bulb. When asked, he said, "I have not failed 10,000 times. I have successfully discovered 10,000 ways to NOT make a light bulb."

Throughout my career as a direct marketer I could have used every obstacle as an excuse not to do it. There were many days when I felt like quitting. One day, I was riding my bike to my car on campus because the parking deck was so far from my dorm. I was wearing a suit and it was snowing. To top it off, some freshman pelted a snowball at me while I was riding. I stopped to see if I knew him, which would have made it okay, but I didn't. I'm sure he forgot all about it, but it bothered me for a while. The irony of it all was that I was on my way to meet with a potential business partner in my downline who was interested in opening our business in a new country! It is inevitable; you will be hit with many snowballs in life. Dodge them or just let them hit the floor, but keep moving.

What obstacles do I need to overcome?

_____

What strengths do I bring to the table?

_____

Where will I need more personal growth and coaching?

_____

These books have helped me tremendously through the tough times. Please take a look at them and allow them to open your eyes to new ideas.

Personal Growth Booklist

1. The Bible
2. *The Greatest Salesman in the World* - Og Mandino
3. *Natural Selling* - Michael Oliver
4. *How to Win Friends and Influence People* - Dale Carnegie
5. *The Business School for People Who Like Helping People* - Robert Kiyosaki
6. *Twelve Pillars* - Jim Rohn
7. *Think and Grow Rich* - Napoleon Hill
8. *The Power of Positive Thinking* - Norman Vincent Peale
9. *Never Eat Alone* - Keith Ferrazzi
10. *Awaken the Giant Within* - Anthony Robbins
11. *7 Habits of Highly Effective People* - Steven Covey
12. *The Strangest Secret* (Audio) - Earl Nightingale
13. *The Automatic Millionaire* - David Bach

14. One-Minute Millionaire – Mark-Victor Hanson and Robert Allen

15. Go For No – Fenton Waltz

16. Success is Not an Accident – Tommy Newberry

Ponder these for when you reach the top level of your company...

What song is going to be playing during your speech?

What are you going to say at your awards dinner?

Are you going to do training sessions for people to show them how you got there?

Do you like receiving recognition for your achievements?

"The problem is not that we aim too high and miss, it's that we aim too low and make it."

— MICHELANGELO

How many lives do you want to change? Directly you can only affect so many, but with your team you can affect thousands, even millions. The more people you help, the more money you make. If you make all the money you need for all your expenses, a nice car and house, would you work a job? Would you spend your time doing something else?

If you don't have a plan, you will be a part of someone else's plan and you might not like it.

Build your dream-life in your head everyday for at least 30 minutes. Picture detailed images in your mind about where you will live, what your house looks like, what your friends and family will look like. What are you driving? Where are you going out to eat? Are you giving back to the community? Are you investing in real estate and other businesses or the stock market? Is your net worth a million? A billion? Are you leaving a legacy for your children and grandchildren? Besides the financial gain, what are you accomplishing for the greater good? Are you having an influence on people? How many? Can you see the small change you are making in the world? How many other people are you teaching to do the same thing? Can you rest at the end of the day knowing you tried your hardest to be the best person you could possibly be?

You can't control others. You can control your own ability to work harder, work smarter, and have a rock solid attitude.

Crab Bucket

Professional crab catchers know that they can catch as many crabs as they can fit in a bucket and not have to worry about putting a lid on the bucket. Why is this? They know that the crabs will only hold each other back. If a brave soul tries to get out of the bucket the others only clasp with their claws and bring the ambitious crab back down to the bottom. So many times this is the case with human beings. We are in a crab bucket by default, but by choice we must leave the bucket. Our family, friends, colleagues, and fellow students act as other crabs trying to bring us down with their "advice." We must separate ourselves from this crowd. That may mean getting new friends. That's okay. We will be living successful lives while they're still living mediocre lives in a crab bucket. Today is the day you can choose to leave the crab bucket, break loose from the chains that others have put on you, and be free. All it takes is one decision. You are fully capable of making it.

"Do for a few years what most people won't so for the rest of your life you can have the lifestyle most people can't."

— WADE COOK

"If you have built castles in the air, your work need not be lost; that is where they should be. Now put foundations under them."

— HENRY DAVID THOREAU

So, what is your next step? Are you ready to make a plan and implement it? If so, send us an email and we will send you an idea of how to start making your plan of action. Email us at DormBasedBusinessBook@gmail.com

About the Author:

Tommy Bryant was born in Lynchburg, Virginia. In 2006, Tommy started his own direct marketing business while still in high school. He moved into the dorm room in 2008, learning through trial and error the ins and outs of building a business on campus. At the age of 19, Tommy reached the highest commission level as the youngest person in the organization to attain it. He is finishing his Bachelor's in Finance at Old Dominion University. Tommy was married to his beautiful wife and best friend in June of 2009.

— NOTES —

— NOTES —

— NOTES —

— NOTES —

— NOTES —

— NOTES —

— NOTES —

— NOTES —

— NOTES —

— NOTES —

— NOTES —

To order more copies of this book, and for large volume discounts, go to:

www.dormbasedbusinessbook.com

or call (866) 637-3853.

Dorm-Based Business Owner apparel and accessories also available, including T-shirts, hats, mugs, and tote bags.

5968747R1

Made in the USA
Charleston, SC
28 August 2010